C

>>> ————————

A MOD

By Mat North

A We Hunt & Gather and Full Court Press collaboration

Coffee: A Modern Field Guide
Second edition printed 2015.

A catalogue record for this book is available from the British Library.

ISBN 978-0-9931148-0-9

Published by We Hunt & Gather
126 Watleys End Rd, Winterbourne, Bristol, BS36 1PP

Every reasonable effort has been made to acknowledge the sources
of information used in this book and contact the copyright holders
of material reproduced. However, if any have inadvertently been
overlooked, the publisher would be glad to hear from the copyright
holders and make good in future editions any errors or omissions
brought to their attention.

Designed by Jon Rich and typeset in Raleway and Garamond.

Cover illustration by Lorna Picton, internal illustrations by Jon Rich
and Lorna Picton.

Printed in Bristol, UK by Taylor Brothers on FSC certified paper.

Acknowledgments

MAT

I'd like to thank Jon for his patience as deadlines whizzed by, Dale, Maxwell, Rosie and Dave for their feedback and Kat for everything.

JON

I would like to thank Lorna, for her unwavering patience and support that has meant the guide became more than a concept and for firmly suggesting I ask Mat to write it. Mat, for believing in the project from the start and going far beyond the role of author.

CONTENTS

Introduction

Welcome to *Coffee: A Modern Field Guide*; a pocket-sized book that's been designed to serve as a quick and handy reference when you're out and about.

Coffee is a vast topic to cover and this isn't intended to be the be-all and end-all of books on the subject, but it will cover everything from the bean to home brewing and all the stops in-between. Along the way, we'll explore how every stage of the production process impacts on the final flavour, helping you to make an informed decision when you order your next coffee or buy a bag of beans to brew at home.

That's quite a bit to fit in, so we're going to move along quickly, packing in as much information as we can. Feel free to dip in and out as you see fit – that's exactly what it's designed for.

Mat North

A little over a year ago, Mat North opened Full Court Press, a small specialty coffee shop in the heart of Bristol. With over 15 years' experience working in the coffee industry, Mat's knowledge and passion ensured FCP quickly became a forerunner in the city's scene.

From the start, Mat's aim has been to help people make informed choices about the coffee they drink. Working closely with a group of trusted roasters, the FCP team can tell you about the traceability of your coffee, often pinpointing where it was grown not just back to the farm, but to an individual plot.

It is FCP's excellent customer service, coupled with the team's ability to articulate their extensive knowledge in an approachable way that has ensured Full Court Press not only serve great coffee, but have sparked an interest in specialty coffee among their customers.

We were lucky enough to listen to Mat talk at a tasting evening held at FCP, where we witnessed his passion and enthusiasm first-hand. From that moment we knew we had found the author of *Coffee: A Modern Field Guide*.

Full Court Press can be found at 59 Broad St, Bristol.

PLANT

WE OFTEN THINK of coffee as a bean, however it's really the seed of a tree in the *Coffea* family. This botanical family contains over 120 different species, but only two are routinely grown for consumption; *Coffea Arabica* and *Coffea Canephora*, known as Robusta.

Coffea Arabica

Coffea Arabica has broad, flat, deep green leaves with a waxy texture. The white flowers are often found on the same branch as ripening fruit.

These two species account for nearly 99% of the coffee grown for consumption worldwide, with Arabica accounting for between 65-80%. Grown primarily in the tropics, Robusta is the hardier variety, growing at higher temperatures and lower altitudes while Arabica thrives in temperate climates and at higher altitudes.

These growing conditions matter. Robusta tends to have simple, bitter flavours and a higher caffeine content to deter pests. Conversely, Arabica and its sub-varieties generally have delicate, nuanced flavours that are often more acidic or floral in tone.

Within each species there are numerous varieties. Some are natural mutations and some

Growing Altitudes

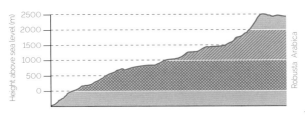

The differing growing altitudes of Coffea Arabica and Robusta

Growing Regions

Tropic of Cancer

Equator

Tropic of Capricorn

Key

Coffea Arabica

Robusta

Mixed

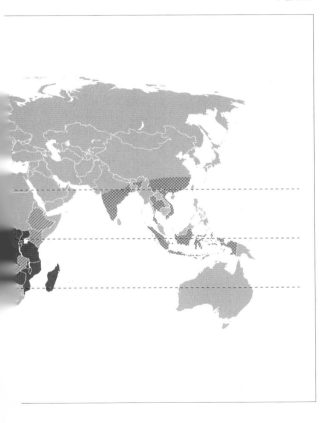

are hybrids grown for yield or disease resistance. Our knowledge of the impact of variety on flavour is still in its infancy, but it is another factor in the ultimate taste.

So which species is best? In terms of quality Arabica has a much higher ceiling, capable of flavour complexities that Robusta currently can't come close to competing with.

Before we move on to harvesting, let's consider why where coffee is grown matters. In other words, lets look at 'terroir'. A term also commonly used when discussing wine-growing, terroir links the ultimate flavour of a coffee to the location and conditions where it was grown. If we look at Arabica through this lens,

Coffea Arabica Varieties

| Typica | Caturra | Catuai | Bourbon | Pacamara | Geisha |

Varieties of Coffea Arabica; these can vary in size and density

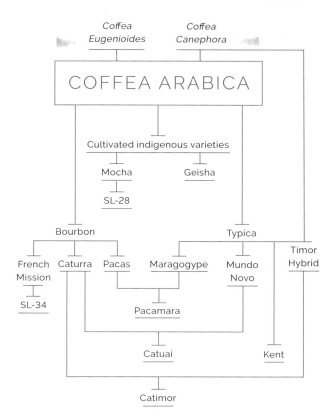

we can see how individual growing countries have reputations for different flavour profiles. Brazil is chocolatey, Colombia is sweet and nutty, Kenya is fruity and Ethiopia, Arabica's native home is floral.

In reality these sweeping generalisations are of only limited use, as increasing traceability and improving quality allow us to see how even individual farms can taste subtly different from their neighbours, and as we'll see, it's all about the taste.

GROW

COFFEE STARTS OFF life as a seed, cultivated in nurseries in the growing countries. It takes between three and five years for this seed to mature into a flowering tree and once or twice a year the flowers mature into cherries, with each tree yielding from two to four kilos.

Coffee Bean Structure

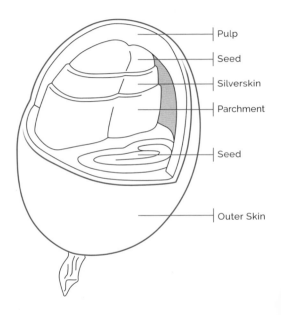

— Pulp

— Seed

— Silverskin

— Parchment

— Seed

— Outer Skin

The internal structure of a typical Coffea Arabica cherry, showing the two coffee seeds in the centre surrounded by their outer layers

Coffee cherries vary in size but have a specific structure. The two hemispherical seeds are surrounded by a thin layer known as the *silverskin*. This in turn has a protective outer layer called the *parchment*. Next, we have the sweet, fruity *pulp* or flesh of the fruit, and finally the *outer skin*. An exception to this is the *Peaberry*, a genetic mutation where the cherry only contains a single seed.

For the best quality coffee, cherries should be picked when fully ripe with a deep red colour and glossy texture. This is easier said than done, as on a single tree cherries will ripen at different times, resulting in branches with fragrant white flowers with both ripe and unripe fruit.

Coffee is constantly being harvested all year round in one part of the world or another, but many countries have one main crop and one smaller fly crop.

Picking methods vary. Brazil's flat landscape and large farms allow mechanical pickers to be used. Known as 'strip picking', this is unbiased and takes every cherry from the tree, from unripe to over-ripe, leading to varying quality.

Coffee Seasons

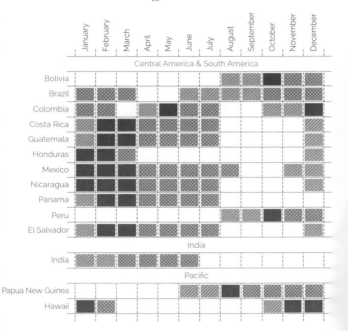

	January	February	March	April	May	June	July	August	September	October	November	December
Central America & South America												
Bolivia								▨	▨	■	▨	▨
Brazil	▨	▨	▨			▨	▨	▨	▨	▨	▨	▨
Colombia	▨	▨		▨	■	▨	▨			▨		▨
Costa Rica	■	■	■	▨	▨	▨	▨					▨
Guatemala	▨	■	■	▨	▨	▨	▨					▨
Honduras	■	■	■									▨
Mexico	■	■	■	▨	▨	▨					▨	▨
Nicaragua	■	■	■	▨	▨	▨						▨
Panama	▨	■	■	▨	▨	▨	▨					
Peru								▨	▨	■	▨	▨
El Salvador	▨	■	■	▨	▨	▨	▨					▨
India												
India	▨	▨	▨	▨	▨	▨	▨					
Pacific												
Papua New Guinea						▨	▨	■	▨	▨	▨	▨
Hawaii	■	▨								▨	■	■

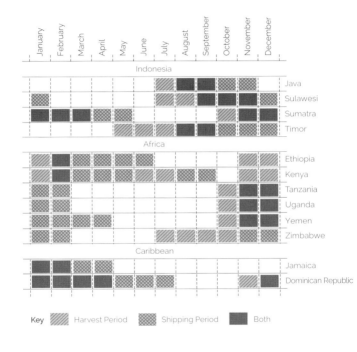

	January	February	March	April	May	June	July	August	September	October	November	December	
Indonesia													
													Java
													Sulawesi
													Sumatra
													Timor
Africa													
													Ethiopia
													Kenya
													Tanzania
													Uganda
													Yemen
													Zimbabwe
Caribbean													
													Jamaica
													Dominican Republic

Key: Harvest Period — Shipping Period — Both

25

The highest quality Arabica is subject to selective hand picking, conducted by trained pickers which ensures a higher proportion of fully ripe cherries are selected. This is more costly as it is labour-intensive and the crop must be picked continuously throughout the season to ensure the maximum yield.

MILL

NOW WE HAVE to turn the freshly cropped cherries into green beans. This process happens at the mills. The *wet mill* processes the cherries, removing the outer layers and revealing the green beans. The *dry mill* then grades and sorts the green beans, finally packing them for shipping.

Wet milling is split into three methods, known as *washed*, *natural* and *pulped natural*. It should happen as soon as possible after harvesting to preserve the quality of the coffee. With care and attention it can allow the inherent qualities of the bean to be preserved; likewise, sloppy processing can ruin even the best cherries.

Washed processing is highly water-dependent, with up to 20 times the coffee's weight in water being used. This results in a cleaner, crisper acidity and more balanced flavours. The process varies from farm to farm and country to country, and results in dried, parchment covered beans with around 12-13% moisture content.

Natural processing is the oldest method and is common in countries with limited access to water. The key difference is that the cherries are dried whole in the sun, using natural fermentation to break down the mucilage covering the bean before dehulling. This fermentation is the cause of the 'boozy' and 'funky' flavours often attributed to naturally processed coffees. Without regular turning of the drying cherries, the process can quickly lead to mould or over-fermentation. Natural coffees exhibit intense fruit flavours, heavy body and sweetness, often at the expense of cleaner and more delicate tones.

Pulped natural processing, known as the *honey process* in some Central American countries, combines properties of both the washed and natural processes. The resulting beans are covered in parchment and have a reddish brown mottling, caused by the drying mucilage. Typically, pulped natural coffees have high levels of sweetness, with a brighter acidity than natural coffees and a heavier body than washed coffees.

After processing, beans are sent to the dry mill. These are often large facilities serving entire regions. Parchment and dried skin is removed to reveal the green beans which are then sorted. Sorting is done by hand or by grading machines, and takes into account size, colour and density while removing defects.

Once sorted, the beans are prepared for shipping. Lower grades are shipped by the container, while higher grades are shipped in bags or boxes and separated by lot.

Processing Methods

NATURAL

Whole cherries are
washed to sort defects
and debris

Cherries are dried on
patios or raised beds

During drying the cherries
are turned regularly to
avoid mould and promote
even drying

After around two weeks
the bright red cherries
resemble raisins. They
are packed and sent to
the dry mill

PULPED
NATURAL

Sorted beans are laid out to
dry on patios or raised beds

Beans are turned regularly
to ensure even drying, this
process lasts 7-12 days

When dry, the parchment
has a mottled red/brown
appearance and the beans
are packed for the dry mill

ROAST

GREEN BEANS ARE packed full of flavour compounds and roasting determines how we experience those aromas and flavours.

Roasting is a skill, and like any skill the key to excellence is how you apply the feedback you gain from testing. So it's no surprise that the best roasters are often the best tasters. The same coffee from two roasters can taste quite different as we are tasting the roaster's interpretation of that coffee.

Roasting is a controlled application of heat to facilitate chemical and physical changes within the bean, the most obvious of these being the colour change. This transition from green to brown is due first to a *Maillard* reaction – a browning reaction between acids and sugar – and then to *caramelisation*, which happens progressively during the roast.

Alongside the change in colour, the most noticeable change is in size and weight. During roasting, beans can lose 12-24% of their weight, but gain in size as the pressure of escaping gases forces them to expand.

SO WHAT HAPPENS IN THE ROASTER?

Once the drum is up to the desired temperature the beans are added, causing the temperature to drop swiftly. Heat is then applied to start roasting; how much heat, and how fast it is applied, is up to the roaster.

Air Temperature During Roasting

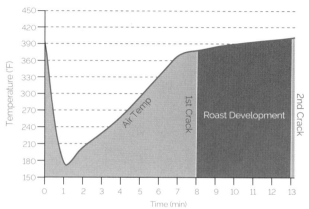

An S-Curve roast profile showing how the temperature in the coffee roaster's drum varies with time

As the beans begin to take on heat and change colour we reach *first crack*. The beans violently eject water vapour and gases, creating a loud popping noise. This is a key point in lighter roasts – the lightest are dropped out of the drum almost immediately after first crack.

Drum Coffee Roaster

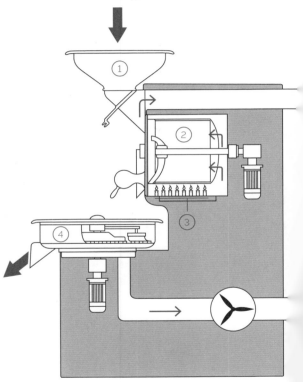

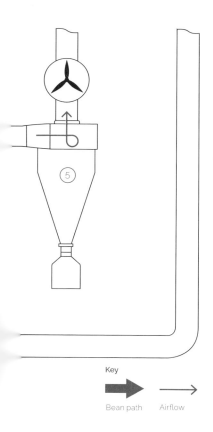

Beans are loaded into the hopper on top of the roaster **1** and into the drum **2**. At this point, the roasting process begins

As the burners **3** provide heat, the drum rotates to avoid scorching caused by lengthy contact with the hot drum wall

After roasting, the beans pass into the cooling tray **4**. Here a fan draws air through the beans to cool them

Hot air passes through the drum and exits via the combustion chamber, passing through a cyclone **5** which removes any debris (chaff)

Key

Bean path   Airflow

The time between first crack and *second crack* – a second popping noise caused by excess CO_2 escaping – is often referred to as the development time. The longer you roast the beans for, the more developed the coffee will be and the darker the flavours will become.

After second crack, oils appear on the surface of the beans and carbonisation begins to occur. At this point, most of the desirable acids and sugars have been roasted away, leaving beans that will taste ashy and bitter.

It's up to the roaster when to stop roasting or 'drop' their beans. On the whole traditional roasts will tend to be darker and longer, while the current fashion is for lighter, shorter roasts.

After roasting, the beans are cooled and sealed in bags with a one-way valve to preserve freshness, then shipped for brewing.

The staling process begins as soon as roasting finishes, however the beans do need time to mature, with 7-28 days after roasting considered the peak window for brewing.

AFTER ALL THE work that has gone into your coffee, you now need to turn it into something delicious to drink.

Like roasting, brewing is about controlling a chemical reaction in the beans, this time by using *osmosis* to extract flavour. In this reaction we use a solvent (water) to dissolve soluble flavour compounds from the coffee. About 28-30% of coffee is soluble, but ideally we want to extract 18-22%. Extraction is hard to measure without expensive equipment, but thankfully there are some flavour characteristics that we can use to help us know when we are in this ideal range.

First, we extract salts and fruit acids. This leaves coffee that is low on extraction, or *under-extracted*. This will taste very tart, sour and tangy, and often a little flat. Next, we encounter the Maillard reactions we saw in the roasting. At this point we are extracting complex sugars which are vital to counteract the acids extracted earlier. Coffee tasted here is at its optimum and should be balanced and sweet, with clear acidity and bitterness.

As we extract further, we move on to dry distillates, or burnt bits. Understandably these don't taste good, leaving the coffee tasting ashy, woody and astringent. Coffee extracted to this level is known as *over-extracted*.

Extraction by Osmosis

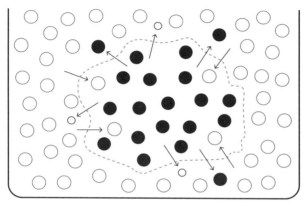

Key

- - - Coffee wall　　◯ Water　　● Coffee　　○ CO_2

The extraction of soluble compounds in coffee happens by osmosis. For this to take place, the coffee must first absorb water whilst ejecting CO_2. Once this has taken place, soluble compounds move from the coffee into the water, from an area of high concentration to low concentration. By controlling the duration of the brew we can control the level of extraction.

Brewing Equipment

KETTLE

TIMER

DIGITAL SCALES

BURR GRINDER   COFFEE

KETTLES can be any shape or size, but swan-neck kettles like the
one pictured allow more control over the water flow

BURR GRINDERS crush the beans between two cut plates. They can
be electric or powered by hand

DIGITAL SCALES are essential for accuracy. Most kitchen scales will
work perfectly but the more sensitive the better

WATER needs to be filtered to remove flavour taints. In hard water
areas you may get better results using bottled water

TIMERS need to measure in seconds, most phones will be fine

COFFEE roasted within 7-28 days is perfect

Brewing espresso at home is a whole book in itself, so for now we are going to focus on brewed coffee, also known as filter coffee, which is easy to achieve at home. But before we get stuck into brewing, what about *buying* coffee? What should you look for?

Information is always good and generally, the more of it the packaging carries, the better. Country of origin, variety, farm name and location, altitude, processing method, roast date, harvest date… all of these can have an impact on the final taste in your cup.

Always look to buy coffee that is within three weeks of the roast date. Coffee is better fresher, but it also needs a little time to mature: as stated previously, 7-28 days from roast is ideal. Ground coffee stales much faster than whole beans losing organic material and ultimately, taste. For the best results, try to buy smaller amounts of whole beans on a regular basis and grind them fresh each time you brew.

Once staling has begun, it's impossible to stop, but we can slow the process by storing our coffee well. As access to both air and light will

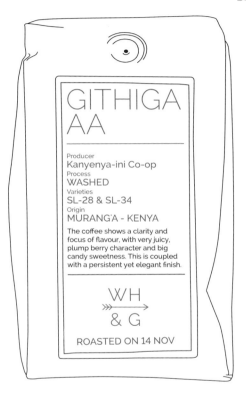

GITHIGA AA

Producer
Kanyenya-ini Co-op
Process
WASHED
Varieties
SL-28 & SL-34
Origin
MURANG'A - KENYA

The coffee shows a clarity and focus of flavour, with very juicy, plump berry character and big candy sweetness. This is coupled with a persistent yet elegant finish.

W H
➤➤➤
& G

ROASTED ON 14 NOV

Packaging design based on Square Mile Coffee Roasters.

COFFEE DOSE

This is known as the brew ratio.
60-70g of coffee per litre of water is a good place
to start for brewed coffee

WATER DOSE

More often than not this is dictated by the size of your
brew method or mug. It works in tandem with your
coffee dose. Always filter your water to remove taints

TIME

This is often determined by your brew method. The
longer the time, the greater the extraction. Once you
have a target time, try to stick to it

TEMPERATURE

Hotter water will extract more quickly, but too hot will
extract too much flavour and vice versa. Aim for 93°C.
Leaving the kettle off the boil for 90 seconds will get
you close to this

GRIND SIZE

Again, this is often dictated by your brew method as
it can control flow in pour-over methods, but it's also
your primary tool for changing your extraction

accelerate staling, use an airtight container and keep it in a dark place. *Don't* store it in the fridge: coffee will easily pick up flavours and aromas from other foods, and you don't want your coffee to taste of last night's dinner!

Before we brew, we need to consider a recipe. Each recipe has five main variables: amount of coffee, amount of water, time of brew, temperature and grind size. All affect extraction. Setting as many as variables as we can before we start brewing means it's easier to make impactful changes based on taste.

The key to brewing is in assessment and then the decisions you make. Try altering one thing at a time and keep a note of what you do.

For example, if your brew tastes burnt and ashy, first check your brew ratio. If it is lower than 60 g/l, raise it and re-brew. Even a change of 0.5g in a 230ml brew can make a huge difference. Similarly, if your grind is very fine, try brewing again with a coarser grind as this will extract less in the same time.

Now we need to pick a brew method. Our variables will be used to control that method.

Aeropress

The brainchild of Alan Adler, inventor of the Aerobie Flying Ring, the Aeropress is an excellent single-cup brewer. Easy to use and to clean, this method is for the Inverted Technique.

WATER   240ml
COFFEE 15-18g
GRIND   Consistency of brown sugar
TIME   2 mins 45 secs

ONE

Insert the plunger into the very top of the Aeropress so it is almost fully out, turn upside down and pour in ground coffee

TWO

Pour in 120ml (120g) of water and start your timer, leave for 30 seconds to 'bloom'

THREE

After 30 seconds add the remaining 120ml of water, leave for 90 seconds. Do not stir – stirring increases extraction

FOUR

During the 90 seconds, rinse a filter paper, place in the cap and attach to the Aeropress

FIVE

After 90 seconds, place the funnel on top of the Aeropress and holding securely flip over onto a jug or cup. Press down lightly and smoothly

SIX

After 30-45 seconds, the plunger should be all the way down and you can drink your coffee

Cafetiere

Also known as the French Press, the cafetiere is capable
of producing excellent coffee when used with care. The
coarse mesh filter allows fine particles and oils into the
brew, giving it body and texture.

RATIO   60-70g per litre
GRIND   Size of instant coffee granules
TIME   4 mins

ONE
Pour in ground coffee

TWO
Add your water and leave for 60 seconds

THREE
After 60 seconds, gently break the crust with a
spoon by pushing down into the coffee

FOUR
Skim any brown scum from the top of the coffee using
your spoon. Place the plunger on top and leave for a
further 3 minutes

FIVE
Push the plunger down slowly and smoothly
to the bottom and serve

SIX
Pour any remaining coffee into a Thermos, left in the
cafetiere it will become overextracted and bitter

BREW

TASTE

TASTING IS ESSENTIAL as it's our key source of feedback when brewing – and our key tool for enjoying a coffee! Like anything, you get better with practice, so the more coffee you taste, the more refined your palate will become and the better you will get at distinguishing flavours.

A cupping bowl and spoon. Any spoon will do but the round shape and deep bowl of a cupping spoon aid slurping and aeration

Professional tasters, or 'cuppers', slurp their coffees using a spoon to aerate the brew and involve all of the taste buds and nasal cavity in the process. This is a little extreme for the home – but it's fun to try!

Using a deep, round spoon (a soup spoon is fine), take a little coffee and bring it up to your lips. Purse your lips and suck the coffee in from the side of the spoon, much like playing a flute in reverse. If you've got it right you should feel the coffee all around your mouth and hear a slurping, whooshing sound. If you're tasting many different coffees, spit the coffee out into a clean cup – if not, just drink it.

Deciding what something tastes like is difficult but you will get better with practice. It's often easier to break it down into sections: front, middle and back.

FRONT

The immediate sensation you get when you taste. This is often the acidity of the coffee. Think about its nature – is it tangy like oranges or sharp like lemons?

MIDDLE

The feel in the mouth that comes after the acidity, known as 'mouthfeel' or 'body'. Is it thick and creamy, or light and delicate? Does it stick to the roof of your mouth, or is it thin like water?

BACK

This is the aftertaste or 'finish', often felt at the back of the tongue. If there is no finish, this is called 'clean'. If there is a finish, is it harsh and bitter, or long and pleasing, like nuts or cocoa?

Tastes and Aromas

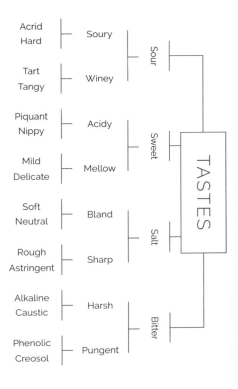

Acrid Hard	Soury	Sour
Tart Tangy	Winey	
Piquant Nippy	Acidy	Sweet
Mild Delicate	Mellow	
Soft Neutral	Bland	Salt
Rough Astringent	Sharp	
Alkaline Caustic	Harsh	Bitter
Phenolic Creosol	Pungent	

TASTES

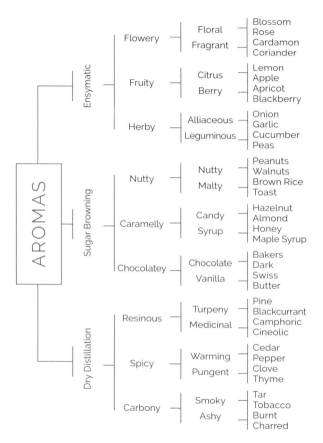

AROMAS

Ensymatic

- Flowery
  - Floral
    - Blossom
    - Rose
  - Fragrant
    - Cardamon
    - Coriander
- Fruity
  - Citrus
    - Lemon
    - Apple
  - Berry
    - Apricot
    - Blackberry
- Herby
  - Alliaceous
    - Onion
    - Garlic
  - Leguminous
    - Cucumber
    - Peas

Sugar Browning

- Nutty
  - Nutty
    - Peanuts
    - Walnuts
  - Malty
    - Brown Rice
    - Toast
- Caramelly
  - Candy
    - Hazelnut
    - Almond
  - Syrup
    - Honey
    - Maple Syrup
- Chocolatey
  - Chocolate
    - Bakers
    - Dark
  - Vanilla
    - Swiss
    - Butter

Dry Distillation

- Resinous
  - Turpeny
    - Pine
    - Blackcurrant
  - Medicinal
    - Camphoric
    - Cineolic
- Spicy
  - Warming
    - Cedar
    - Pepper
  - Pungent
    - Clove
    - Thyme
- Carbony
  - Smoky
    - Tar
    - Tobacco
  - Ashy
    - Burnt
    - Charred

Tasting diagrams are useful to draw the links between what we sense and what we think it tastes like. Often a coffee won't taste exactly like strawberries or caramel, but have the characteristic acidity or sweetness that remind us of them.

There are no rights or wrongs to tasting and no-one's suggesting you have to think about every coffee in this way. But it can only add to your enjoyment if you learn to discern the delicate flavour and balance that is available to us in the highest quality coffee.

Acidity   Taste associated with extracted acids, usually linked to fruit flavours

Aroma   Smell of the dry coffee grounds

Ashy   Tasting of burning or charcoal, much like the taste of burnt toast

Astringent   Harsh and drying acidity

Bitterness   Often acrid and unpleasant. Bitterness can however also be a positive when balanced – tonic water is good example

Back   The end of the taste, usually attributed to the finish, eg "really clean at the back"

Body   Sensation of weight or viscosity. Espresso is thick and has lots of body as opposed to brewed coffee which is light in body

FLAVOUR GLOSSARY

Bouquet   Smell of the wet coffee grounds and drink

Bright   Describing acidity, clear and intense

Buttery   To have a thick, buttery mouthfeel

Chalky   Having a dry, grainy mouthfeel or finish

Clean   Little or no finish

Complex   Coffee with many levels of flavour

Drying   Slightly drying acidity, think cranberries

Finish   Describing the end of the taste

Front   Immediate sensation upon drinking

Furry   Wet, fuzzy mouthfeel

Lingering   Long finish

Middle   Sensations of sweetness and body during drinking, eg "syrupy sweetness in the middle"

Mouthfeel   A compliment to body, eg "it has the mouthfeel of cream"

Sharp   Distinct pointed acidity, like lemon juice

Silky   Smooth, luxurious mouthfeel

Sourness   Acidic in nature but often linked to fermented flavours or dark fruits, eg cherries

Syrupy   Sweetness or texture like sugar syrup

Tangy   Rounder acidity, elements of sourness

Thick   To have lots of body

Thin   Lacking in body, watery

Woody   Stale taste of old beans, like a wooden stirrer

Zesty   Floral acidity, think of orange zest

LIST OF ILLUSTRATIONS

All About Coffee WH Ukers

The Blue Bottle Craft of Coffee J Freeman, C Freeman & T Duggan

Coffee Basics K Knox

Coffee Flavour Chemistry I Flament

Coffee Obsession A Moldvaer

Coffee with Tim Wendelboe T Wendelboe

Espresso Coffee: Professional Technique DC Schomer

Espresso Coffee: The Science of Quality A Illy & R Viani

The Espresso Quest Instaurator

Everything But Espresso S Rao

Finca Tamana T Wendleboe

God In A Cup M Weissmann

Left Coast Roast H Neuschwander

The Professional Barista's Handbook S Rao

Uncommon Grounds M Prendergrast

The World Atlas of Coffee J Hoffmann